ALASKA

Copyright © 1988 Raintree Publishers Inc.

A Turner Educational Services, Inc. book. Based on the Portrait
of America television series created by R.E. (Ted) Turner.

Library of Congress Number: 87-26487

12345678910   9291908988

Library of Congress Cataloging in Publication Data

Thompson, Kathleen.
  Alaska.

  (Portrait of America)
  "A Turner book."
  Summary: Discusses the history, economy, culture,
and future of Alaska. Also includes a state
chronology, pertinent statistics, and maps.
    1. Alaska—Juvenile literature. [1. Alaska]
I. Title. II. Series: Thompson, Kathleen. Portrait of
America.
F904.3.T46   1987   979.8—dc19   87-26487
ISBN 0-86514-471-0 (lib. bdg.)
ISBN 0-86514-546-6 (softcover)

Cover Photo: Michael Gordon

★ ★ ★ ★ ★
Portrait of AMERICA

ALASKA

Kathleen Thompson

A TURNER BOOK
RAINTREE PUBLISHERS

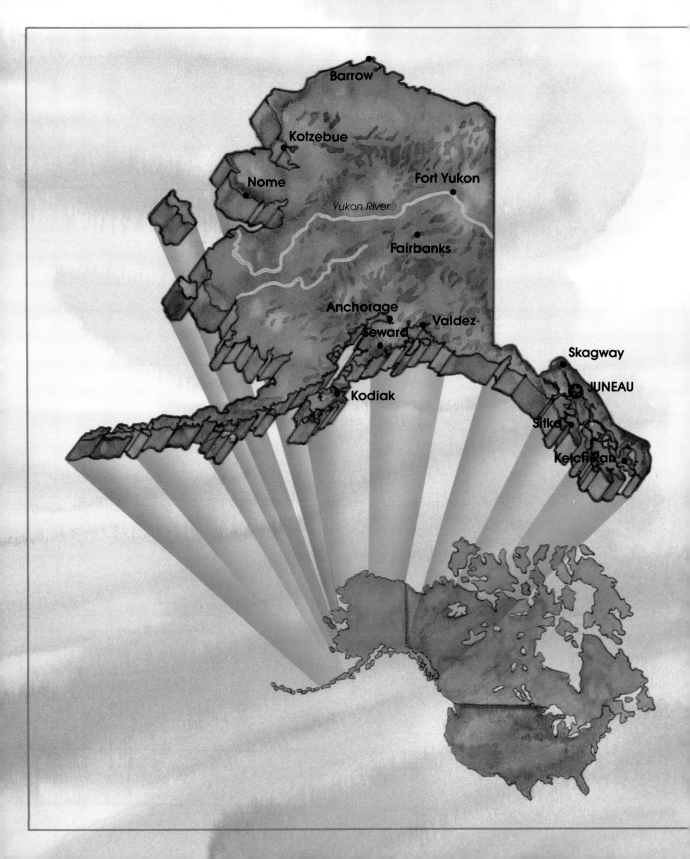

CONTENTS

Introduction   7

Land of the Northern Lights   8
   The Eskimo Way   20
   Living in the Back Country   24

Seward's Gold Mine   28
   On Track   32

Northern Arts   34
   Born to the Water   40

Opening the Frontier   42
   Important Historical Events in Alaska   45
   Alaska Almanac   46
   Places to Visit/Annual Events   46
   Map of Alaska Counties   47
   Index   48

Introduction

Alaska, the Last Frontier.

"I've had some pretty hairy experiences where I was caught out there, and survival was tipsy, but I wouldn't trade it for anything."

Alaska: wilderness, pipeline, trains and totem poles, the fewest people and the most volcanoes.

"I don't know. There's something here that's just nowhere else I've ever been. You can be in a world of absolute splendor and the next day you're up to your knee bones in snow and wind."

Some people say that Alaska is the most magnificent state in the Union. Most would agree it's the coldest. It's a place where bears still take charge of a river. It's also a place where you can walk into a four-star hotel in Anchorage. It's a place where the back country is so remote that towns get their food and medicine by airplane. And where the biggest oil strike in the nation got every Alaskan a check in the mail.

Alaska. You have to see it to believe it.

A bighorn sheep in one of Alaska's National Parks.

Land of the Northern Lights

Alaska is really the place where America was discovered. It is the most ancient of all the Indian lands. Alaska was the place where Asian tribes first crossed over to settle in North America.

Archaeologists believe that Asians crossed the Bering Straits sometime during the last Ice Age. They were probably hunters who came following game. Archaeologists disagree on the dates, but they think it may have been between 15,000 and 25,000 years ago.

There are several groups of Indians who are still living in Alaska. Then, there were many. Along the southern panhandle were coastal Indians, such as the Tlingit and Haida. They lived in small towns on the rich land by the sea. They

At left: Tlingit Indians.

Above: a native of the Aleutian Islands, the first part of this state explored by Europeans.

were hunters and fishers. During the winter they devoted themselves to culture and recreation. They were outstanding carvers, woodworkers, and weavers. Every birth, marriage, death, or initiation was celebrated with a huge party know as a potlatch, where huge amounts of food and other property were given away to the guests.

The Aleuts were a sea-going people who lived mainly on the Aleutian Islands. They were sea hunters, who fished and hunted whales and otters. Far to the north were Eskimos, who lived along the coast and inlets of the Arctic Ocean. They, too, hunted whales and otters from small boats.

The first European to come to Alaska was a Danish sea captain, Vitus Bering. He was sent by Czar Peter of Russia in 1725. At that time, very little was known about the area around northeast Asia and the northwestern part of North America. Czar Peter commissioned Bering to find out if Russia was connected to North America.

This was no small assignment. First, Bering and his crew had to travel 6,000 miles across Russia and Asia. Then, when they finally reached the peninsula of Kamchatka on the Pacific Ocean, they had to set out to sea. They built a ship and by 1728 they were ready to sail.

They sailed north and reached St. Lawrence Island, which is now part of Alaska. They continued north and went through the Bering Strait. They did not see the Alaskan mainland because of fog.

Bering made a second voyage in the summer of 1741. This time he was joined by the Russian explorer Aleksei Chirikov. Bering explored the mouth of the Copper

River and landed on Kayak Island.

That November, Bering and his crew were shipwrecked on their way home. The crew was stranded on an island for almost a year. During that time Bering and thirty others died. The others built a small boat and finally returned in September 1942.

This second expedition brought back one exceptional thing—sea otter furs. No one in Asia or Europe had ever seen sea otter furs. The furs were sold at the market in Canton, China, and they brought the largest price ever paid there for furs.

The news spread quickly. Soon the Aleutian Islands were overrun by Siberian hunters trying to make a quick fortune. The native Aleuts, isolated from each other on different islands, were often killed or enslaved. The Siberians fought with each other over furs. The peace of the islands had been destroyed.

Soon news spread to the rest of the world that Russians were interested in the northwestern coast. The English, Spanish, and French sent ships into the region.

At left: Vitus Bering. Below is a cathedral built at Sitka by the Russians.

Spain had long before made a claim to all the Pacific coast north of Mexico. In 1775 they declared that their claim included the Alaskan coast.

The famous English explorer, Captain James Cook, arrived with an expedition in 1776. He was there to look for the Northwest Passage. At that time, the only way from the Atlantic to the Pacific was around the tip of South America. Many explorers

Below: Gregory Shelikof is shown with a Russian Orthodox church at Kenai, the second-oldest Russian settlement in America.

USDA Forest Service

Alaska Purchase Centennial Comm.

tried to find a northern route.

Captain Cook sailed along the coast as far as the Bering Strait. When he couldn't find a passage, he and his crew collected furs to sell in Canton. Then they spent the winter in the Hawaiian Islands. That winter Captain Cook was killed by Hawaiian natives.

His ship returned the following year under Captain Clerke. This time they made it as far as Point Lay. As they turned back, the crew nearly mutinied. They had made so much money on furs the first time, they wanted to stay and keep hunting. Captain Clerke was barely able to keep them in control.

Several years after the Cook expeditions, Gregory Shelikof became the first Russian to settle in the Alaskan region. He set up a fur trading post on Kodiak Island in 1784.

Meanwhile, Spain was ready to assert her claim. She sent ships to Alaska in 1787 to find a good place to start a settlement. They chose a site near Nootka. When the Spaniards returned the next year, they found the English already there. The Spaniards seized the English ships, almost

starting a war with England. By 1792, Spain was forced to give up its claims on Alaska.

The English continued to work on their Pacific holdings. Captain George Vancouver further explored the northwest coast, charting many of the islands and inlets.

Meanwhile, the Russians reinforced their claim to the region. In 1799 they chartered the Russian-American Company to bring the fur trade under control.

The company's first manager was Alexander Baranov. Since the Russian-American Company was the only governing organization in Alaska, Baranov was the governor of the whole state. He ruled for the next eighteen years.

The company's headquarters was near Sitka. Under Baranov's management, the Russian-American company made a lot of money.

Baranov treated the natives— both the Indians and the Aleuts— very badly. His treatment led to an uprising by the Tlingit that resulted in the massacre of the Russians and the destruction of Sitka. The town was rebuilt two years later.

Above is the check for $7,200,000 used to purchase Alaska from the Russians.

Baranov retired in 1817. The Russians who took over the Russian-American Company did not seem interested in operating the company or in Alaska. The company's business decreased. For one thing, because of all the hunting, herds of otters and other fur-bearing animals were decreasing. Also, competition from British, Canadian, and American trading companies was cutting into the Russians' profits. In addition, Russia was involved in a war from 1853 to 1856. All these factors worked together to make Russia anxious to sell Alaska.

Negotiations between Russia and the United States began but were delayed by the Civil War. Finally, in 1867, Russia made a formal proposal. Secretary of State William Seward agreed, and the United States paid Russia $7,200,000. That amounted to about two cents per acre.

Even though the price of Alaska was extremely cheap, there was a lot of opposition to the purchase. Some people felt that having Alaska was useless, when there was still a lot of good farmland in the western United States that had not yet been settled. Some newspapers called the purchase "Seward's Icebox" or "Seward's Folly."

At this point Alaska was still pretty wild. At the time of the sale there were very few Europeans living in the entire territory. The coastal Indians were still powerful and aggressive.

Now that America had bought Alaska, no one quite seemed to know what to do with it. It was under the rule of the War Department, but it was pretty much left to itself. In 1877 the last soldiers left the area.

The local Indians got to be so threatening that the Americans at Sitka had to ask for a U.S. warship to protect them. When a warship didn't come right away, they sent to Vancouver to plead for a British ship. Finally the British did send a warship to protect the town until an American ship could arrive.

For a long time, Alaska attracted not farmers but fishermen. The coastal waters were rich in salmon and other fish. The first canneries were built in 1878.

In 1884, congress passed what was called an Organic Act. It established Alaska as a district with laws (although they were the laws of Oregon) and a court system. A school system was also established.

Large companies set up hunting and fishing syndicates. As a result of their activities, however, the numbers of some animals began to dwindle. Before long otters, walrus, salmon, and whales in the area were threatened. The natives' lives depended on these animals. It was at this time when native Alaskans began

Commercial fishing was one of Alaska's earliest industries. Below: a day's catch of crab.

Skagway during the Yukon Gold Rush.

to use reindeer as a source of food.

Gold had been found in Alaska in the 1860s and in 1881. But in 1896, large deposits of gold were discovered in the Klondike. That is in the Yukon Territory of Canada just across the border. The gold strikes attracted thousands of people. The only way to get to the Yukon is to get to Alaska by ship and then travel overland. A number of towns, including Skagway, were founded in Alaska as a result of all the people traveling to the Klondike.

The gold rush in Canada had barely ended when gold was discovered in Nome and in Fair-

banks—in 1899 and 1902. The resulting gold rushes there brought many new people to Alaska. The increase in population encouraged Congress to pass more laws. In 1899, a code of criminal laws was established. And in 1900, civil laws were passed.

The gold discoveries caused the United States to take another, more positive, look at Alaska's potential. In 1906, Alaska was allowed its first representative in Congress. Democrat Frank H. Waskey was elected. He was allowed to speak in Congress, but because Alaska was not a state, he could not vote on issues.

Attention was again focussed on Alaska in 1910. Gifford Pinchot—the head of the Forest Service—accused Richard Ballinger —the secretary of the Department of Interior—of giving forest land to big business groups. Their dispute became known as the Ballinger-Pinchot Affair. Ballinger was cleared, but it became obvious that Alaska's natural resources were being abused by business groups. It was clear that Alaska needed more governing. In 1910, Congress firmly restricted the hunting of otters. In 1912, Congress passed another Organic Act. The act made Alaska a United States Territory, and a territorial legislature was set up.

In 1916 copper was discovered in Cordova. There was a boom that was even bigger than the gold strikes for a while, but the mines only lasted until the 1930s.

After the gold rush period, the population had dropped. Once again the economy relied on fishing, mining, and fur trading. The Alaska Railroad was completed in 1923. This linked Seward and Anchorage on the coast with Fairbanks in the interior.

In the 1930s Alaska worked to develop agriculture. Farming had never been a major industry in Alaska. Now, with government aid, farms were established in the valleys near Fairbanks.

Above: Alaskan farming in the early part of this century. Below: a team of horses is used to haul the locomotive "Dinky" to Riley Creek during the building of the Alaska Railroad.

17

The Alaska Marine Highway is a state ferry system.

When World War II broke out in 1941, the country realized how important Alaska was. It stretched out into the Pacific, close to China and the Soviet Union. The United States began to develop military bases in Alaska and built the Alaska Highway to help keep the area open.

In 1942 the Japanese attacked several of the Aleutian Islands. They captured the small islands of Agatta, Attu, and Kiska. The United States recaptured them again early in 1943. They were the only parts of North America, in which there was fighting in World War II.

After the war the military continued to build up in Alaska. Military bases were enlarged, and radar systems were set up across the territory.

By 1959, Alaska was ready for statehood. It became the forty-ninth state. The first year of statehood was expensive, however. Alaska had to take over the cost of maintaining its own schools and road systems. In 1963 and 1964 Alaska tried an innovation in transportation. It opened the Marine Highway. This was a state ferry system, to link towns along the coast.

In 1964 Anchorage and Valdez were hit by the biggest earthquake ever recorded in North America. What was more, the earthquake caused a huge sea wave that destroyed a great deal of property along the coast.

A few years after this, Congress decided to settle a long-standing problem in Alaska — treaties. The native people of Alaska had not collected all that was due to them from old treaties signed as the land was settled. Now Congress approved the granting of over $960 million and forty million acres to fulfill treaties from the early days.

Then there was another big strike in Alaska. This time it was oil. Oil was discovered at Prudhoe Bay in 1968. It was a giant oilfield, believed to be the largest in North America.

It took some time to decide on how to transport the oil. Some people wanted a pipeline, but others thought that might damage the tundra, the kind of land special to Alaska. Finally it was decided that a pipeline was the best idea. The Alaskan pipeline took three years to finish, but, finally, in 1977 the pipeline was completed and the Alaskan oilfields were ready to produce.

Later, Alaska moved to protect more of its great riches—its wilderness. In 1978 President Jimmy Carter set aside more than fifty million acres for the National Park System. Two years later Congress passed the Alaska National Interest Lands Conservation Act. They preserved another 100 million acres. Altogether, almost one-quarter of the entire state is now protected land.

Alaska is still rich in natural resources. In the past, some of that wealth was carelessly exploited. But now, Alaska is in control of its destiny.

Building the Alaskan Pipeline. The work was completed in 1977.

The Eskimo Way

"The history of America is that Native Americans lose their land and are constantly assaulted with respect to their self-determination and their own culture. That's a sad history."

Paul Ongtooguk is an Inupiaq Eskimo, and he's tired of the same old story. He wants a different story for Alaska.

In some ways Alaska is already different. Eskimos still have their villages, although the villages have changed. They still have their land and the sea. They've had to fight very hard for what they have.

Above: classes at Kotzebue. Paul Ongtooguk (right) teaches a course in Native Studies. His students are finding solutions to their own problems by studying the culture of their ancestors.

20

Courtesy Paul Ongtooguk

"Even if you're not hunting on it (and most Alaskan natives are) and even if you don't derive a good part of your food off of that land (which most Alaskan natives are doing), it's important to know that it's still there, and that it's still ours."

The village of Kotzebue had to learn that lesson the hard way. A few years ago, it was facing some very serious problems—alcohol,

Rick Furniss / AlaskaPhoto

drugs, family violence. Something had gone wrong.

John Schaeffer was the mayor of Kotzebue. He set out to find out what was wrong and how to fix it.

"So we went through a process of trying to evaluate what happened, talking to experts—psychiatrists, psychologists, those kinds of people—and really didn't come up with anything."

That's when the mayor of Kotzebue decided to turn to another kind of wisdom. He went back to the culture of his people.

"We were holding elders' conferences at that time, and we asked the elders. And basically they said that the problem was that values of the Inupiaq were not being taught to our children."

Now at Kotzebue they're working on those values. They're teaching the young ones who they really are. Because they can't afford ever to forget.

Paul Ongtooguk would say that Kotzebue has learned a lesson in history.

"Traditionally, elders have played a tremendous role in how native cultures were governed, taking the wisdom of age and applying it to your more pressing problems."

The challenge in Alaska today

is to use the wisdom of the past to find a way into the future.

"Here, in Alaska, we're trying to be optimistic that the three-hundred-year legacy of conflict between Western society and Native American will somehow turn out different. Alaskan natives have the opportunity to become another downtrodden minority, or we have an opportunity to create a very successful synthesis between our own society and that of Western society."

These pages show Eskimo traditional culture. Above: men sing and play the tambour. On the left-hand page: a woman spearfishes. Major General John Schaeffer, former mayor of Kotzebue, is pictured at right.

my life? It's exactly what I'd been looking for and didn't know it."

You could call Jay Hammond

Living in the Back Country

"I was not one of those who as a child or youth aspired to come to Alaska. Never thought much about it. And I found when I crossed the border to Alaska the first time, it was like coming home for the first time. I thought, gee, where has this been all

Jay Hammond (above) served two terms as governor. Right: in the backcountry, where there are no runways, a float plane can make a landing on any available body of water.

the ultimate Alaskan. He's been a fisherman and a bush pilot. He's even been elected governor. Now he's back living on his land near Bristol Bay. Alaska is his state, and he loves it.

"Things are etched in more vivid colors. We live in extremes. We're the farthest north, the coldest, the smallest communities, the biggest state. You know, everything's in superlatives."

Some of Jay's best memories are from the years, when he was a bush pilot. Bush pilots fly passengers and supplies to remote places that could otherwise not be reached. Sometimes they have to land on glaciers or mountaintops. And they have to fly in all kinds of weather. It's a dangerous profession. But to Jay, the beauty more than makes up for the danger.

"It's spiritual, sustaining. It blows the cobwebs out of the soul, to see that sort of wilderness panorama unfold beneath you. People coming here, I think, feel compelled to live a life or have an attitude which is a different. You're living on the edge, on the cusp of survival versus nonsurvival. Just the fact that you've lived through the day is exhilarating."

For Jay Hammond, Alaska is the joy of wilderness. It's the joy of adventure in a world that's become too tame. It is the joy of having wide-open land, and all the challenge in the world. And it's the joy of being strong enough

On the left-hand page: Jay Hammond with his airplane. Above: a landing at Mount McKinley.

to meet that challenge. That makes all the hardships worthwhile.

"I think Alaska, in the minds of many, still constitutes a dream of sorts. There seems to be enough of that Alaskan mystique remaining that persons find once they've come here it's very difficult to live elsewhere."

That's understandable. There's nowhere else like Alaska.

Seward's Gold Mine

They once called Alaska Seward's Folly. That was before the Gold Rush. And Alaska has been proving people wrong ever since. After the Gold Rush, copper was discovered, and it became as important as gold. Then, in 1969, oil was discovered in Prudhoe Bay.

Oil is still a big part of the Alaskan economy. In the years the Alaskan pipeline was being built, 1974-1977, jobs from the pipeline were the single largest source of personal income in the state.

Now the pipeline is finished and oil is flowing through it. But oil hasn't turned out as well as people had hoped. In the late seventies, Alaska residents were getting tax breaks from the oil profits and even direct payments from the state. But by

The 800-mile-long Alaska Pipeline.

the mid-1980s, oil prices had dropped substantially and the oil boom had ended. Overall, mining accounts for about one-third of the gross state income. Fortunately, Alaska's economy doesn't depend exclusively on oil. Alaska has natural gas. There are rich deposits near the Cook Inlet—where there is also a lot of oil.

Gold can still be found at the old gold strikes and various other parts of the state. However, most of the gold that can be mined economically has already been taken from the ground. For the most part, it is not worth mining the gold unless the price of gold is very high.

The list of minerals in Alaska goes on. One of the most important tin deposits in North America is near the town of Lost River. The state also has good amounts of sand and gravel, coal, iron, barite, mercury, platinum, and copper. In addition, there are smaller amounts of antimony, nickel, silver, tungsten, and uranium. Alaska was hardly Seward's Folly. It was Seward's Treasure Chest.

Alaska has a thriving fishing industry. In the cold coastal waters are some of the richest fishing areas in the world. Salmon is the most important catch. In fact, salmon makes up two-thirds of the total production of the fishing industry. Ships also harvest king crabs, halibut, and shrimp.

Service industries play a major

The people of Alaska have tried to develop their state's oil resources without bringing harm to the wildlife here. An oil drilling site and a caribou are pictured below.

ARCO Alaska, Inc.

part in the Alaskan economy. They contribute about half of the gross state product. The government and military contribute twelve percent of the total. The federal government is the single biggest employer in the state. Alaska is in a strategic military location, and there are a great many military bases.

Agriculture provides a very small part of the state gross product. The growing season is short, but with long daylight hours of summer, plants grow very rapidly. Most cool-weather vegetables can be grown up to the edge of the Arctic Circle. The majority of the farms in Alaska are near Anchorage. Today, three-quarters of the farm products of the state come from this area.

Livestock consists of some cattle, hogs and pigs, sheep, and poultry. Most of Alaska's livestock, however, are reindeer. Reindeer are adapted to cold weather, and have no trouble grazing on the land.

Reindeer are just one more Alaskan solution to Alaskan conditions.

Alaska Division of Tourism

On Track

"The conductor's the boss of the train. First of all, his main thing is to get the train from point A to point B without hitting any other trains."

Steve Culver is the boss of this train. He's the conductor on the Alaskan Railroad.

The line was built in 1923 and it mostly runs through wilderness forest. Sometimes the train has to stop for bears or caribou. Sometimes it has to stop for Alaskans.

If you want to get on the Alaskan Railroad, you don't necessarily go to a train station. There

Above: conductor Steve Culver loads passengers at Denali National Park. At right: Steve is shown with a view of a bridge crossing at Riley Creek.

aren't many train stations along the line. There is just too much land and too few people. So you just have to flag down the train.

"You just step up next to the tracks and wave back and forth, and the engineer'll give you a couple of toots when he sees you.... We pull right up like a taxicab and spot the train right alongside them. They load everything in the baggage car, jump on the train and away we go."

The atmosphere is friendly on

the Alaskan Railroad. Many of the people who ride it live in the back country. The train gives them a chance to socialize. It's one of their few chances to chat with their neighbors, since their neighbors may live 400 miles down the tracks.

The train services towns, villages, and groups of cabins too small even to be called villages. There aren't any highways out there. In some cases, there's not even a real road to the train track.

"They tell me when they get on where they want to go. They'll say, 'I'm going to 238.4.' And over the years, I know 238.4 is a bridge, there's a trail off the side of the bridge and there's several cabins in back, as far as twelve miles back."

Alaska. There's no other place like it. And there's no other railroad like the Alaskan Railroad.

Northern Arts

The art of Alaska is the art of the Indians. Native culture is still alive and producing art in Alaska. And a lot of Alaskan art can be seen in museums around the world.

The Tlingit Indians of the southern panhandle had a coastal culture. The climate was temperate and rainy, and the Tlingit were prosperous. They lived in clans. Each clan had a different animal. Some Tlingits might be of the eagle clan. Others might be bear or whale. They used these symbols throughout their art.

The Tlingit carved beautiful totem poles with many different symbols. The totem poles were often made to celebrate important events or to help the Tlingit remember stories. Sometimes the Tlingit's totem poles showed their sense of

A totem pole at Ketchikan.

humor. After the United States purchased Alaska, Secretary of State Seward went there to inspect the area. The Tlingit had a potlatch in his honor. A potlatch is a celebration during which gifts are exchanged. For some reason, Seward did not give the Tlingit gifts. They were insulted. So when they carved a totem pole of Seward, they made his appearance very unflattering.

Each Tlingit clan had at least one important lodge. The posts of the main house were elaborately carved and painted. Inside, on the back wall, there were cedar planks. The planks were carved with the history of the clan. The storage chests were also beautifully carved and painted.

Their art usually reflected everyday objects. They might, for example, make names into poetry. For example, a girl might be given a name like "Sunshine Glinting." Her father might be from the Killer Whale clan, so that had to be part of her name, too. Her whole name might become "Sunshine Glinting on the Dorsal Fin of the Killer Whale as It Rises."

Totem poles and carvings are shown on these pages. Below: a Tlingit clan house. Top of left-hand page: a totem pole for America's bicentennial.

The Anchorage Symphony Orchestra is pictured above.

Another name might be "Raven Flying Out to Sea Cawing in the Early Morning."

The art of the Indians has given Alaska a rich cultural heritage. It is a heritage that is shared with the Eskimos. Native designs are seen today in all kinds of art, including oil painting, wood carving, weaving, and pottery. That native art is often displayed in art shows in Nome, Fairbanks, Juneau, and other towns.

The Eskimos who live in the north often carve sculptures in soapstone, which is found near the seashore. Sometimes the artists carve in ivory, which is obtained from walrus tusks. The sculptors carve familiar figures, often the animals they hunt.

Alaska is also becoming home to mainstream American artists and musicians, who find inspiration in the wilds and the cold. Anchorage has a symphony orchestra, and internationally known concert artists tour the state in the winter.

Alaska Division of Tourism

Joel W. Rogers

Top: a native woman weaving a basket. Below: a ceremonial costume of the Tlingit Indians.

Born to the Water

"I was born into it. My father and my mother are fishermen. I was born in Cordova, and if you live in Cordova, you fish. It's not a question that ever even occurs to me. It's something I do. It's like the salmon, I guess. They return every spring. They can't help it."

Some of the best fishing in the world is in the waters off Alaska. Sylvia Lange runs a fishing boat in Prince William Sound. It's her boat and her crew. And all her crew are women. Sylvia was surprised that anybody would bother to make an issue of it.

"Well, I didn't think having an all-female crew was going to be any sort of big deal. I mean, I just selected the people that I wanted to be on my crew, and they turned out to be female . . ."

Other people didn't look at it that way.

"This one fellow came up to me and said, 'I heard you're going to have an all-female crew this year.' And the first question I get asked is 'Who's the engineer?' And so I said, 'Well, I heard you had an all-male crew. Who's your cook?'"

What's important is that the work gets done. Fishing isn't an easy job. It means being out in all kinds of weather. It means being able to fix it yourself if anything breaks, because you're an awfully long way from the nearest hardware store. And it means staying out until you find the fish. Fishing can be a wonderful life or it can be the exact opposite.

"It strictly depends on if you catch fish or not. You're out there to catch fish, and if you're not doing it, you're not doing what you're there for. It's not even like you make the association with money. Money is something that comes up at the end of the season. But when you're doing it, the reason you're there is to catch fish, and if

you're not catching fish, it's not excit- ing. You've blown it."

There's something else special about the life. There is the beauty of the islands. Sylvia Lange has come to realize that the work is only part of her life at sea. She also remembers to appreciate what's around her.

"You can't just pursue fish. Fish- ing is a part of this place. I don't think once I'm out fishing that I'm one of *these people who ignore everything else, because I love Prince William Sound. It's beautiful. And I will notice that the hemlock trees are exception- ally beautiful—and there's enormous hemlock trees on Night Island—and that there's wildflowers growing in the lichen cliff above Sun Harbor. . . . If you do this for a living, it's half your life. And you can't get so busy that you don't stop and notice the world around you."*

On the left-hand page is skipper Sylvia Lange. Sylvia's fishing boat is pictured below.

Opening the Frontier

Alaska is a land of potential. Alaska is a land of frontiers—unexplored regions, unknown resources, untapped wealth. Even today, no one really knows what is in Alaska. The vast oil field at Prudhoe Bay was only discovered in 1969. Many areas have never been tested because it is so difficult to get the people and equipment in to test them.

Alaska has vast coal resources but one working coal mine. Alaska has a land mass equal to one-fifth of the continental United States and one major railroad line. Alaska has more of everything and less in use than practically any other part of the world.

Yet some parts of Alaska have collided with "civilization" too hard, too fast. Fur hunters nearly wiped out the sea otters.

Glacier Bay National Monument.

Above is a seal in a wilderness area.

Fishing fleets pushed the whales and the walrus to the edge of extinction. And with the wholesale slaughter of sea animals, the native population whose living depended on the animals was nearly destroyed.

But Alaska is a land of survivors. The sea otters and the walrus have come back. The sea otters are now legally protected, and international agreements protect the whales as well.

The Native Americans have fared better in Alaska here than in many other parts of the United States. Alaska was not colonized as fast as other states were. The Aleuts, Indians, and Eskimos were hit hard by the first waves of Europeans. But they had time to recover. Now they are rein-forcing their own ways of life. The rest of the country has finally come to realize that the native cultures of this country are a part of our heritage that none of us can afford to lose.

Alaska is still a frontier. Americans have finally learned to value frontier. Americans have begun to harvest resources while respecting the integrity of the land.

Alaska has much of its development ahead of it. It stands to benefit from all the mistakes the other states have made. Alaska still has its wilderness, still has its wildlife, still has much of its native culture intact. Alaska, with all its riches, can be a place where progress doesn't have to go wrong.

The city of Anchorage is pictured below.

Important Historical Events in Alaska

1728 Vitus Bering explores the Bering Strait and lands at St. Lawrence Island.

1741 Bering sets out on a second expedition with Russian explorer Aleksei Chirikov. They landed on Kayak Island.

1778 The British send Captain James Cook to Alaska to search for the Northwest Passage.

1784 Gregory Shelikof becomes the first European to settle in Alaska, on Kodiak Island.

1792 Spain is forced to yield all claims in Alaska to the British.

1792-1794 Captain George Vancouver makes a detailed exploration of the Alaskan coast.

1799 Russia charters the Russian-American Company to control fur trade. Alexander Baranov is made manager.

1802 Tlingit Indians wipe out Fort St. Michael in Sitka.

1818 Baranov retires. Russian naval officers take charge of the Russian-American Company.

1824 Russians sign a treaty with United States, setting boundaries and allowing trading rights.

1825 Russians sign a treaty with the United States, setting boundaries and allowing trading rights.

1861 The charter expires for the Russian-American Company.

1867 Secretary of State William H. Seward buys Alaska from Russia.

1878 The first canneries open in Alaska.

1884 Congress passes the first Organic Act, which gives Alaska a legal code.

1896 Gold is discovered in the Canadian Klondike.

1897-1898 Gold prospectors pour through Skagway into the Yukon Territory.

1899 Gold is discovered at Nome.

1902 Gold is discovered at Fairbanks.

1903 A border dispute develops between Canada and the United States. A commission decides the disagreement in favor of the United States.

1906 Frank H. Waskey is elected the first Alaskan delegate to Congress.

1912 Congress passes the second Organic Act, giving Alaska a territorial legislature.

1916 Copper is discovered at Cordova.

1923 The Alaska Railroad is completed, linking Seward, Anchorage, and Fairbanks.

1942 The Japanese invade the Aleutian Islands of Agatta, Attu, and Kiska. The Alaskan Highway is completed.

1959 Alaska becomes the forty-ninth state.

1964 The worst recorded earthquake in North America hits Anchorage and Valdez.

1968 Oil is discovered at Prudhoe Bay. It is believed to be the largest oilfield in North America.

1971 The U.S. Congress passes the Alaska Native Claims Settlement Act. This resolves long-standing treaty disagreement in Alaska.

1977 The Alaskan pipeline is completed.

1978 President Jimmy Carter sets aside over fifty million acres in Alaska as part of the National Park System.

Alaska Almanac

Nickname. The Last Frontier

Capital. Juneau.

State Bird. Willow ptarmigan.

State Flower. Forget-me-not.

State Tree. Sitka spruce.

State Motto. North to the future.

State Song. Alaska's Flag.

State Abbreviations. Alas. (traditional); AK (postal).

Statehood. January 3, 1959, the 49th state.

Government. Congress: U.S. senators, 2; U.S. representatives, 1. **State Legislature:** senators, 20; representatives, 40. **State Divisions:** 23.

Area. 589,757 sq. mi. (1,527,464 sq. km.), 1st in size among the states.

Greatest Distances. north/south, 1,200 mi. (1,931 km.); east/west, 2,200 mi. (3,541 km.). **Coastline:** 6,640 mi. (10,686 km.).

Elevation. Highest: Mount McKinley, 20,320 ft. (6,194 m). **Lowest:** sea level, along the Pacific Ocean.

Population. 1980 Census: 400,481 (32% increase over 1970), 50th among the states. **Density:** 1.5 persons per sq. mi. (0.58 persons per sq. km.). **Distribution:** 64% urban, 37% rural. **1970 Census:** 302,583.

Economy. Agriculture: barley, hay, silage, potatoes, lettuce, milk, eggs. **Fishing Industry:** salmon, shrimp, king crabs, halibut, snow crabs. **Manufacturing:** fish products, lumber and wood products, furs, stone and clay products. **Mining:** oil, natural gas, gold, sand and gravel.

Places to Visit

Alaska Highway, between Dawson Creek and Delta Junction.

Denali National Park.

Glacier Bay National Park.

Katmai National Park and Reserve. "Marine Highway," state ferryliner system.

Pribilof Island.

St. Michael's Russian Orthodox Cathedral in Sitka.

Annual Events

Alaska Arts and Crafts Show in Juneau (March).

Anchorage Fur Rendezvous (February).

North American Championship Sled Dog Races in Fairbanks (March).

Mount Marathon Mountain Climbing Race in Seward (July).

Russian Festival in Kodiak (August).

State Fair in Palmer (August-September).

Alaska Day Festival in Sitka (October).

Alaska Counties

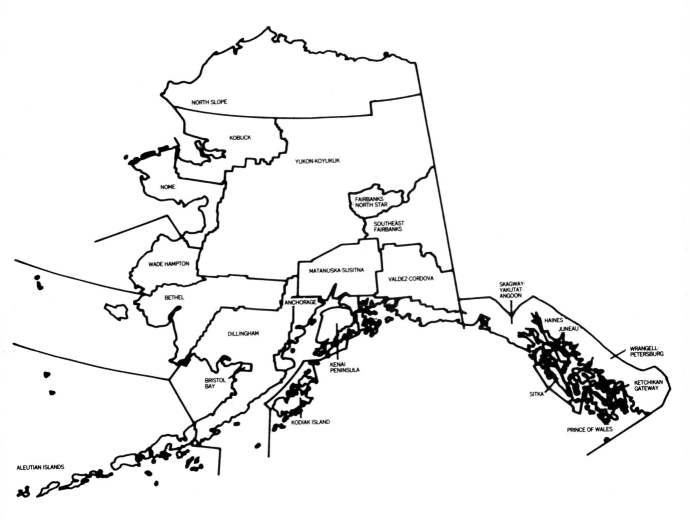

NORTH SLOPE

KOBUCK

YUKON-KOYUKUK

NOME

FAIRBANKS
NORTH STAR

SOUTHEAST
FAIRBANKS

WADE HAMPTON

MATANUSKA-SUSITNA

VALDEZ-CORDOVA

BETHEL

ANCHORAGE

SKAGWAY-
YAKUTAT-
ANGOON

HAINES

JUNEAU

DILLINGHAM

WRANGELL-
PETERSBURG

KENAI
PENINSULA

KETCHIKAN
GATEWAY

BRISTOL
BAY

SITKA

KODIAK ISLAND

PRINCE OF WALES

ALEUTIAN ISLANDS

INDEX

Agatta, 18
Alaska Highway, 18
Alaskan pipeline, 19, 29
Alaskan Railroad, 17, 32-33
Alaska Territory, 17
Aleutian Islands, 10, 11, 18
Aleuts, 10, 11, 44
Anchorage, 18, 39
Attu, 18
Ballinger-Pinchot Affair, 16
Baranov, Alexander, 13-14
Bering, Vitus, 10-11
Bering Strait, 13
canneries, 14
Carter, Jimmy, 19
Chirikov, Aleksei, 10
Cook, James, 12-13
Cordova, 17
court system, 14
culture (of Alaska), 35-39
earthquake, 18
economy (of Alaska), 29-31
Eskimos, 10, 20-22, 39, 44
Fairbanks, 16, 39
fishing, 14, 30, 40-41, 44
fur trade, 11, 13, 43
future (of Alaska), 43-44
gold, 16, 17, 29, 30
Haida Indians, 9-10
history (of Alaska), 9-19, 45
Juneau, 39
Kamchatka peninsula, 10
Kayak Island, 11
Kiska, 18
Klondike, 16
Kodiak Island, 13
Kotzebue, 20-22

laws, 16
Marine Highway, 18
mining, 30
National Park System, 19
natural resources, 16, 19, 30
Nome, 16, 39
Nootka, 13
Northwest Passage, 12
oil, 19, 29-30, 43
Organic Act, 14, 17
otters, 14, 17, 43, 44
Point Lay, 13
population, 16, 17
potlatch, 10, 36
Prudhoe Bay, 19, 29, 43
purchase (of Alaska), 14
reindeer, 16
Russia, 13, 14
Russian-American Company, 13-14
salmon, 14
school system, 14
Seward, William, 14, 36
Seward's Folly, 14, 29
Shelikof, Gregory, 13
Sitka, 13, 14
Skagway, 16
St. Lawrence Island, 10
statehood, 18
Tlingit Indians, 9-10, 35-38
totem poles, 35
treaties, 18-19
Valdez, 18
Vancouver, George, 13
walrus, 14
Waskey, Frank H., 16
whales, 14
World War II, 18